CHASING EVIL

CHASING EVIL

FELIX NORTHWOOD

CONTENTS

CHAPTER 1

Introduction

While living in Oregon in the late 1970s, I was assigned to the Oregon State Penitentiary. Among the inmates I worked with was a man named Jerry Brudos, who had been convicted of murdering four women. Jerry Brudos was a sadistic and lethal type of psychopath: a sexually sadistic serial murderer. This type of serial killer enjoys humiliating, torturing, and finally destroying their victims. Each of Brudos's female victims had been snatched off the streets of Portland, where they were missing persons for months before their lifeless bodies were discovered in a state of sadistic mutilation. One of these victims was the only daughter of a Spanish-American family. She was little more than a child when she was snatched from her mother's apartment in Portland and transported to the state penitentiary's morgue. This case that involved Jerry Brudos became my first experience with sexually sadistic serial murderers. After all these years, and of all the violent criminals I have confronted, I still remember the deep and unimaginable sorrow etched in the faces of innocent family members. Innocent family members are often as much the victims in such serial-murder cases as the person who is finally tortured and murdered by the killer.

This heartless pursuit of innocent and beautiful young women within our human ilk is not just brutal and unfathomable. It is truly evil. For as renowned photojournalist Bill Mckeen wrote of such evil: "Evil is always there, and It hurts sometimes more than we can bear". However, popular culture often distils complex mysteries into binary stories. The police hero/serial killer demon dyad. Many true crime books are written to create excitement and satisfy a public craving or fear of monsters who live in our midst. This book's true crime roots are uniquely rich and rare: one of the co-authors, journalist Jack Olsen, corresponded with the happy-face serial killer, Edward "Ed" Kemper, while Kemper was stalking the streets of Santa Cruz. Jack learned that even "the Co-Ed Killer" was evil in different ways, but also that meaningful and valuable secrets could be-as Jack hoped—wrung from this killer's wicked thoughts. During a recent phone conversation, Jack Olsen told me that he did not publish all of Ed Kemper's disclosures because he did not want to provide "...a manual on being a serial killer". That, he said, would only entice more into committing these heinous and soul-destroying crimes.

CHAPTER 2

Understanding Serial Killers

Few depravities exceed those of serial killers - murderers who kill repeatedly for the most base of motives. They offer the ultimate nightmare: faceless, unknown, they may strike anywhere, at any time, their selection diluting to randomness the reassurance offered to people who are careful where they go or who they allow into their houses. Every city possesses its secret lost youths, and every police department its files bulging with unsolved homicides. These men and women savages are not legendary demons. As real as you or me, every so often they sweep into view, presenting investigators with crimes whose incomprehensible brutality marks them as far beyond what society would consider tolerable.

Despite the fact that 85 to 90 percent of all homicides are committed by relatives or acquaintances of the victim, people who have grievances and disagreements and who kill in emotional arguments quite often depending on drugs or alcohol or both, the majority of both fiction and non-fiction books, movies, and television programs with a homicidal theme focus on the dozen or so cases a year involving serial killers. The press calls them the bad news.

And who are they? Are they called us to reluctantly acknowledge a different line of thinking, because anybody capable of such behavior must be different in some very basic ways from the remainder of the population? Or to the horrified delight of the ghouls and voyeurs among us, who feast on the knowledge that these killers may have clubbed one of us? Who are these savages? What do we think we know about them?

Psychological Profile

Based on research on the relationship between environmental scarcity and violent conflict, I would like to propose the following psychological profile of our dangerous psychopath. I will call this individual for now Challan. The primary personality trait I would expect from such a person would have to be a high degree of emotional detachment from his environment and his (potential) victims. This would allow Challan to carry out the crimes without feeling any emotional sentimentality toward his victims, and would facilitate his continuous hunting of humans. This opens up the rather unsettling possibility that such a dangerous character would not necessarily have to be emotionally disturbed. Most people, for example, also have emotional detachment toward insects. The difference is one of quantity.

A second matter to consider is the necessity of a great emotional stability, provided Challan would not be considered emotionally disturbed. The primary reason is that such a continuously thrill-seeking character would have to keep himself constantly entertained with these immensely dangerous and thrilling actions of feigning civilization. If he were not constantly entertained and fulfilling that desire for his extremely dangerous pursuit, his latent character traits would certainly reveal the true person behind the mask authoring the leather-bound diary, behind the pretty and tame-looking façade, and we would have quite a different person on our hands.

Behavioral Patterns

The FBI's Criminal Investigative Analysis Program or BAU employs analysts to produce psychological profiles of unknown offenders involved in especially heinous violent crimes. The profiling process employed by the analysts of the FBI consists of consulting with investigators to obtain background data on the case, studying the crime scene, and examining the forensic evidence left by the subject. Orientation of the offender with the investigative team's primary investigative response plan analogy begins with a careful review of the information presented.

Because of the obvious need for constructive speculation, presumptuousness, and resultant inconsistency in criminal investigations, including profiling procedures, these should be regarded not as substitutes but only as supplements to traditional investigative methods. The profiling process deployed by the Federal Bureau of Investigation comprises four separate steps consistent with the logical process that should be followed in developing profiling: (i) profiling inputs; (ii) decision process models; (iii) crime assessment; (iv) review of criminal profile or investigative suggestions. The profilers who work within the Federal Bureau of Investigation are few in number and cannot be expected to work every unresolved and infamous murder case submitted to them. They select the cases where background information is valid and readily available, where reliable resources exist to assist them in disseminative tasks suggested by the profile, and where the results of the investigation will likely corroborate or disprove their construct.

CHAPTER 3

The Evolution of Forensic Science

In the late 1800s, getting caught up in a murder case was definitely not good for one's career or one's social rectitude. As a popular song of the time went, "An unfortunate man is Mr. Muste, who murdered his cousin and ate him with mustard. He especially loved to eat kim with mustard." Most murders were never solved in that long ago time. If the murderer had money or position, he could often just disappear and that would be the end of it. A few people exonerated at the last minute were buried alive. Yes, people were dead who should have been alive, and alive who should have been dead. It was a ghastly situation that, along with much additional monstrous sordidness, would never have been replaced with the semblance of what we now know as "modern civilization" if religious belief had not been dying out rapidly but had lived on to see the end of the Edwardian era. The century was fit for vast experiments both good and bad, and its unwilling peoples were put to the test. The test came.

The end of the century comported with our later image of horse racing being fixed, and, in a way, it was. But since all life begins at the wrong end of the century, there was bound to be a strong measure of inevitable hopelessness overarching all the end-of-the-century nonsense. The ways of collecting evidence about homicide, rape, arson, robbery, and major theft were so violent, costly, and unsatisfactory as to produce tears of outrage and pain. Then a new science was born: forensic medicine. It was very slow coming but came. It walked onto the stage grimy with blood, choked with ignorance, and very poorly dressed. This new girl soon learned that her beribboned colleagues could dance for a time, as did the Entertaining Spectacle, and an emphatic time it was. She also discovered that few of her new friends were worth a tinker's dam, and since then she has given calm and cool reappraisals to many of her fair-weather friends. Women of her kind are often brought out for parties and more often than others are asked to leave in a hurry. Science, like a singer, a woman pushing a pram, or a longshoreman, has a time to learn, a time to blossom, and a very specific time to fade away. It had been a terrible time. It could only get better. And so it did; at times. Since investigators like her, certainly no beautiful winner prancing arrogantly in scorn before prideful international judges, have evolved slowly and sometimes seem to have gone off in many haphazard directions, the many who have dazzled the public have gained its ready acceptance. If, by losing herself to adopting the wishes of others, she becomes something she can never be and will always be less than she really is—then should she accept the mortifying situation and join the bashful world around her? (In case you wondered, I am giving a brief, very subjective introduction to the growth of forensic medicine before the arrival of a method for discovering blood, then to that method itself.) As it came to pass, forensic crime detection did get better. When certain worthy professionals began beating the bushes for evidence, they soon discovered that they had found nothing new, for there was no scientific foyer for them to walk into. They wanted to know, "How do you trace down a particular bloodstain?" "How do you find out whether a dried stain is blood, and then make absolutely sure?" "Who can tell us how to get blood out of various fabrics, anyway?"

Early Techniques

In the early twentieth century, anthropologists were concerned with racial classification rather than crime analysis. Conklin writes, for example: "After examining many crania of numerous tribes that existed at various times, we are at a loss to find any reliable morphological character which will distinguish the physical aspect of civilized or uncivilized people." In other words, a person's physical characteristics could not tell a scientist which race he belonged to. Similarly, once the police began collecting other types of physical evidence (photographs, personal documents, fingerprints), their repositories were filled with data that were of no practical value. But over several decades, fingerprinting has proven to be an infallible means of identifying humans much more reliably than physical appearance.

The early methods were coined "function police identification" and are illustrated in Fig. 3.1. Police manuals listed the following intrinsic features of the ear that could be classified: prominence, curvature, and attachment (point of meeting with head). These are either inaccurate, not unique, or complicated to measure, and as Conklin, who worked with these techniques, pointed out, could be altered by "the transient states of the muscles, such as fright, intense reflection, laughter, anger, and the constitution of one's health".

Modern Advancements

Modern-day procedures are rekindling hope that there might be resolution in some of these older cases. The use of mitochondrial DNA technology on the remains of some of these long-at-large murderers was tried recently by a major law enforcement agency. The new DNA testing seemed to indicate that the long sought killer might have been some random truck driver specializing in driving around random cities along the east coast. Rapes and other crimes in these other cities that yielded similar DNA samples were also being searched through and DNA samples for a number of truck drivers who happened to be driving through stricken cities at the time of the rape were being sought. As of the writing of this chapter, no such arrest is known to have resulted from this questioning of the truck drivers, and no update on the case is available.

It seems likely that if an arrest does result from this question, or if some other high profile criminal case's forensic issues result from using mitochondrial DNA in the manhunt, law enforcement agencies will be more open to the idea of retesting the stored remains of many of the FBI's most wanted convicted offenders to see if such technology will work in the cold case investigations of those long dead serial killers. No one knows if modern advancements will do the job; but it is very interesting to think that they might. These long cold cases (as of the time of the writing of this chapter) include: Altemio Sanchez, who is at large for a number of unsolved rapes in the Buffalo, New York area; Robert Fisher, wanted for the murder of his wife and their two children in Scottsdale, Arizona; Glen L. Godwin, an escapee from Folsom State Prison who mutilated and killed his former cellmate; and Jose Fernando Corona, wanted for the asphyxiation murder of a South Gate, California man.

CHAPTER 4

Famous Serial Killer Cases

The question used to be, "Who was Jack the Ripper?" but today no one seriously entertains the idea that the question will ever be answered. By contrast, American analysts, from self-proclaimed experts to the leading academic criminologists who have developed a viable profile of both serial murder in general and its archetypal perpetrator in particular, regularly clash over the substantive details of the hunt for other giants of the abyss. What of women who kill for suffering's sake? The first documented American serial killer? They receive wide exposure to the crime-loving American public. Yet America's vanishing giant, my vetoed Maus, virtually unknown, consumes my mind.

On internet postings, write-in candidates batting .166 or worse predict the utter failure of police to apprehend this country's first "world-class" killer. The American dread accompanying the election of Jack the Ripper or Anarchist violets. Recently liquidated, their stakes have passed to the once resplendent, 32-year investigation of the Linda DNA murders. Are the police really better today, or shall this case consolidate center stage in the debate between hunters and those critiquing them and their premiers?

Jack the Ripper

The Jack the Ripper case is the granddaddy of all homicide-fatigue experiences. At least in modern times. The citizens of London in the year 1888 suffered a short and violent attack on their peace of mind. On consecutive mornings, the bodies of prostitutes began turning up in the same square mile of Whitechapel. The crimes stood out because of the manner in which each victim was killed. The slasher was unrestrained. He slashed throats, eviscerated and mutilated, usually while still in a drunken rage, it seems. The murderer was never captured. There were many suspects, but none were arrested and successfully prosecuted.

In the centuries that followed, many killers would claim the mantle of Jack and commit similar crimes. Several were actually caught. Today, we think of the Ripper as a pathetic pervert who had an acute psychotic episode, during which he murdered five women (disregarding the consensus of contemporary police, physicians and the public that the Ripper's savage assaults on the victims occurred as post-mortem indignities). But the Ripper case still fascinates ordinary citizens, Whitechapel district preservationists, Ripperologists, movie makers, authors, and historians. Just last week a court in Wales found a postman guilty of "the Ripper diary hoax," which had netted him some neat pocket change, and sentenced him to a sentence of eight years.

Ted Bundy

Perhaps no serial killer in history has attracted as much influence from the popular press as the late Theodore Robert Bundy, and possibly no other has managed to create more controversy in the depiction of their crimes. Bundy has proved to be an enigma; he was intelligent, with little relevant criminal history, and yet clever enough that he was able to kill so often and easily victimize his targets. His smarts, undeniably good looks, and satanic-like charisma all endeared him to a wide variety of people.

In a time when much Hollywood fare has become filled with special effects, artful celluloid depictions of violent serial killers have become commonplace. When real life presents us with the tape recording of the voice of a sick, demented, psychosexual killer of women, the tapes have become a favorite subject in forensics classes, making Bundy a legend in his own mind. This is a man who became famous in Victorian Florida, thumbed a ride from a sitting governor, murdered a woman, sleepwalked through his first trial and trial preparation with Anita Larsen, killed again, escaped custody, was arrested and highlighted the importance of dental odontology and microscopic hair examination evidence in his trial, defended by O.J. Simpson lead counsel Johnnie Cochrane, developed a relationship with porn actress Kimberly Kyle who left her husband to be with him and may have first refuted his guilt in preferring his porn star lover to a career as a dedicated legal assistant, called his mother to bail him out and got a bank president to guarantee the million-dollar bail on his re-captured bond, acted as his own attorney with co-counsel Judy Clarke, was convicted of three brutal sex murders that occurred on consecutive Saturdays in one northern Florida town, was convicted of murder in two other states, requested exploitative photographs of child murder victims to defend himself in reflecting his grief at the death of Megan Kanka, the daughter of Holmdel, New Jersey, neighbor, took longer than either of the Tate-LaBianca killers to be executed, sired a child with his wife while on death row and married her prison sidekick, Charlene Shellnick, the phase II response of women prisoners to a man who murdered 12 women in Oregon, Idaho, Utah, Colorado, and Florida, may have tried to find another woman's footprint in a room he burgled, a most unlikely example of a necrophilic killer. Without him, the urging of defense experts, no.

The press did not make Bundy the icon that he became; the law enforcement people did that. The FBI provided detailed information of his brutal sexual crimes and his "killing kit" dated 1976 and the North Carolina sex offenses, Florida investigators worked tirelessly to solve Bundy's crimes, but it was the southeast U.S. press that gave Bundy the attention he so badly wanted. It was the press that first labeled him the "Cascade Casanova". The press continued to feed Bundy's ego, frequently publishing material that he "leaked" to them. They seemed delighted to publicly dance to their own piper, and their love affair with Bundy flourished. Newspapers and television news kept the drama of Bundy's escapades alive. For five years, the newspapers and television newscasts of the nation reran the grisly story of Bundy's series of love and death. Without Bundy, or Bundy's good buddy, the press has to find another paragon of virtue and evil, so that the sick and deranged can continue to vicariously "Jenny Craig" the acts the average John and Jane does not dare think about. With Bundy's departure, the public was left thinking what a grand homecoming this had been, benefiting seemingly nobody.

CHAPTER 5

Law Enforcement Strategies

Detection and apprehension of a serial sex killer is not easy. Whereas there are certain common characteristics of a typical homicide and certain highly successful techniques used to solve these cases, the five major categories of serial killers do not share these characteristics. Since the five templates are based upon the presence of a sexual component, it is obvious that law enforcement strategies must never place a lower priority upon the cause of death and whether or not there was sexual overkill. This motivated component in the homicide opens up options available to and utilized by the local police investigator.

The Brett Law line of interrogation and the police intelligence gathering techniques of the United Kingdom can develop a suspect list, or lists, over a short period of time upon the place of business, study, or worship of a lot of persons. The unique feature of the sexual component in the serial sex homicide is that it tells not only the 'who' of the perpetrator, the determining location of a suspect pool, but it also gives the 'why' of the murder, allowing local law enforcement to get into the mind of the killer prior to the act while he is cooling off, realizing that he will have to come to the same place to kill again.

Task Forces

Modern-day serial murder investigations are generally conducted by a joining of federal, state, and local law enforcement personnel, all working together to solve these hideous crimes. To describe how effective and efficient the joining of all these disparate resources can be, the classification system must explain both its structure and its function. This depth of operational detail is essential, as solving murders is the ultimate mission in any law enforcement entity. The commitment of personnel and resources will influence the process. Task forces have become essential in today's criminal justice umbrella. Very few successful complex investigations are not conducted by these multi-discipline joining of forces. These are investigatory entities formed by federal, state, local, and sometimes even international entities. They pool all of their various resources to successfully resolve the criminal behaviors attributed with local impact and influence.

Many major cases are frequently coincidentally solved when local federal authorities open an investigation parallel to the local police activity. Major cases are meticulously monitored for their influence on law enforcement resources, social concerns, sensational and shocking import, and investigatory resources inherent. District Attorneys, City Attorneys, and U.S. Attorneys must frequently coordinate and cooperate with law enforcement in these necessary communities of interest task forces. These need to be career-oriented professional entities. Their commitment and goals are met by certifying law enforcement entities that demonstrate through their work efforts, results, resolution, and prosecutorial skill and mission a commitment to collaborate, share, and join forces in support of community interests that go beyond the scope of only their particular local responsibilities and jurisdiction.

Profiling Techniques

Hunting patterns are important to law enforcement because they are a potential key to understanding the behaviors of predators. Game hunters can accurately predict the prey hunting habits of predatory animals, whereas a conscientious predator can, by intelligence and forethought, outwit the game hunters. This issue of the game playing back at the hunters is the essence of the problem of catching serial killers and is well understood in the military, among other professions. The concept of hunter-hunted reversals is a vital tool for understanding and dealing with dangerous situations, where there are two smart adversaries, one elite, specialized, and intensively trained and highly skilled, and the other devious, unpredictable, and often more highly motivated and more cunning.

Dennis Rader, the BTK strangler, murdered ten people in Wichita, Kansas, before being arrested by an old-fashioned detective, in large part because Rader was a bumbler, arrogant, stupid, and too casually certain that law enforcement would never capture him. Rapid decisions under stress can easily mask hindrances to efficient operation and allow serious obstacles to defense to remain unaddressed. Such failures may have devastating consequences, especially in ones that can have a profound effect on the national and individual psyche, such as the serial murder of children. The question many non-government groups, self-help organizations, and policy makers are interested in is, "Can something other than the wing-and-a-prayer mode of catching a bad guy be used to prevent serial killers from going on a murder spree, and can the techniques the military and government organizations have developed offensively as well as defensively aid in stopping these predators?"

CHAPTER 6

Media Portrayal of Serial Killers

The way that media portray serial killers has a significant impact on popular culture. There is tremendous interest and fascination with the crime and criminal. Some sources argue that media accounts of particularly horrific crimes can inspire copycat offenses. The media has the power to tell the public what to think about and then how to go about thinking about it. If the public is told and shown the actions and results of the activities of a group or individual that falls far outside the lines of acceptability, negative emotional reactions are a wearisome result with a public relations return assured.

There are over ten thousand sources of varying media continuously disseminating information on the subject and reporting film and television production can only serve to escalate public attention and interest. Those involved in various aspects of film and television production take advantage of the public's accelerating interest in particular crimes by creating and developing investigative and dramatic themes. Some actors have exaggerated the character of sexually perverted murderers and killers in order to sell tickets and advance their own careers. Terminating some of these actors' careers could put a halt to that approach. Hollywood would lose interest in a subject and this would be another medium in which no one would care to work. Without sensationalism, there would be no box-office draw on any given weekend.

Movies and TV Shows

These movies and TV shows cover types other than my suspects, but the fact that they are murderers and horrible killers is not the point. What makes my "suspects" different is that they have a body count of known victims. This count not only includes the murder of 29 known male victims, but some claim to have had 110 victims, and others even more. Even at the bottom of the scale, that easily exceeds the number of victims. I was supposed to be executed on March 5, 2010, for these historic criminal activities, but I was ill in the hospital when that was scheduled and have never heard what kind of proofs they used exclusively that fit all of these murders. What made this the worst unsolved crime ever committed by anyone was that the first of the heinous murders could be determined in September 1962. This was when she acquired the upstairs apartment across the street with a perfect view of him and his activities. She used this view for many years every day thereafter. On August 13, 1974, she acquired the house.

True Crime Podcasts

The people in the true crime community we connect with on social media, the podcasters who bring unimaginable acts of violence into our daily lives, regular people who read and write about unsolved cases, are all here for pretty much the same reason as the people who thermographically search for buried bodies. We love a mystery. Human beings have an innate desire to solve puzzles.

Podcasts are the secret to that elusive work-life balance, taking the most mundane daily tasks and turning them into the plot twists we once found time for between thick covers. Now we download a story nominally related to whatever we were doing before we pressed play. Work out next to a journalist solving a murder. Housework alongside a criminal defense attorney exonerating the wrongfully convicted. Get lost on the commute home with a narrator revisiting inhuman cruelty. Okay, that's a mishmash of personal playlists, but in most cases, we're in pursuit of a mystery.

CHAPTER 7

The Impact on Victims and Families

Of all of the hidden or only partly understood problems of serial murder, the helplessness, fears, and rage of the families of the victims stand out dramatically. The family of the victim has, perhaps, a harder time than the victim himself at the hands of society. Not only have mothers lost their loved ones, but at times they are called on by the police, the press, and society to give information to find the killer. In an effort to do their part, many mothers made contacts with people living in the areas where killings occurred. They posted their children's pictures; some slept poorly with the phone nearby in case it rang. In some cases, there was so much fear it was found to be very difficult; however, all tried to be very diplomatic in formulating questions. These family members have fought long and hard battles to help bring information to light. It was only through their efforts, courage, and sacrifice that this work was possible.

As stated earlier, many of the victims didn't have parents or did not live with their parents. There were mothers who had left their children in the hands of other people. In turn, there were the people who simply dumped their own responsibilities. Unfortunately, over 60 mothers who are alive today have lived those feelings of guilt with a pain worse than death. The war is not over as far as the family members of the victims are concerned. Not only did they lose the primary relationship because of murder, but it also seems they were unable to speak. In general, one of the functions, if not the first function of the family, is to protect its members. While the most noble and the most beautiful symbol of God is supposed to be the family - the joy, the shelter, the warmth, and the care of those in the family depend on an individual's struggle with himself so it can be possible to overcome his problems. In particular, the family is supposed to protect those members who are poor, feeble, defenseless, and helpless against the world. It is the task of the family to protect the sick, the elderly, children, sick animals, and weak members. The family also seems to be the place where individuals can develop their abilities and skills.

CHAPTER 8

The Ethics of Studying Serial Killers

When it comes to a discussion of serial killer victims, criminologists are on solid ground in asserting that more information about victimization helps to prevent subsequent victimization. This is one of the underpinnings of crime prevention. However, where this argument falls on its face is when it comes to the study of the psychology of serial killers. Virtually everything that is published about a serial killer is material he, as a rule, provides imagining that this material furthers himself in some meaningful way, gratifies him in some fashion, is eloquent and convincing. In effect, society's indulgence of the acting out and confidences of serial killers is based on the proposition that these murderers have something to tell us about life and human nature. To assume that serial killers have much to offer in terms of a psychological view and a valuable analytical lens is to elevate and commingle the considerable power they believe their acts confer and the brutal anti-social personae they develop to establish and express their beliefs about power. That McElroy's public sexual tortures of females has nettled him is arguable, but it can also be argued that the boasting, showboating, and self-aggrandizement so common to serial killers are not indicative of seriously disrupted minds continually vexed by fierce internal struggles.

This blend of cunning and savagery that is so integral to so many serial killers can repel ever so much more than it captivates and instructs. At the same time, every society (and democracy) worthy of the name must recognize that it can never entirely renounce the pursuit of the exact truth about man, whether that is disclosed by art or science, whether that may be an exhilarating or a tormenting process. This is most assuredly not an argument for star-chamber or some other secret deliberations or a "total case" approach to certain crime studies. It is to argue, however, that what is perceived as the subjective judgment of responsible people, making as disinterested a search as is humanly possible for what has happened, what people are like, the lessons that should be drawn from a harrowing event, is a part of what sustains a society and enables it to progress. We must not ignore any effort that aids our understanding, accurate and kind understanding, of what human beings are capable of doing to one another in an effort to achieve or maintain or enhance power.

CHAPTER 9

International Perspectives on Serial Killers

Serial killers are a worldwide phenomenon, and some countries appear to be prime breeding grounds. Motivated by commodification (selling of goods with serial killers' images), political motivations (fear control, morality, voting), economic incentives (solutions), and/or ideological purposes (blaming foreign influences), the number of foreign serial killers has been exaggerated. Up to 85% of all serial killers reported as foreign-born outside the U.S. kill in their adopted country. Little research is available which studies international serial killers within their native country (in contrast to international killers outside their own country). The problems of defining and identifying serial killers within culturally diverse settings were explored in an informal survey of 105 international and 20 U.S. experts. Cultural-specific aspects unique to international settings were identified. A case study was used to illustrate the promise of addressing culture-specific issues. To make the claim that Israel has a much higher concentration of serial killers than other countries would seriously bias the data unless such a population was truly factual, although this cannot be denied.